Hertfordshire's Lost Railway

by
Keith Scholey

After closure to passengers the Hemel Hempstead branch saw several rail tours. Here, the South Bedfordshire Locomotive Club visits 'the Nickey' at Hemel Hempstead on 24 September 1960.

ACKNOWLEDGEMENTS
The publishers wish to thank the following for contributing photographs to this book:

John Alsop for pages 3, 8, 10, 12, 16, 23, 24, 27, 29, 34, 35, 37, 38, 42, 45, 46 and 47; R.M. Casserley for pages 2, 4–7, 9, 11, 13–15, 17, 18, 21, 22, 26, 28, 30, 31, 33, 39, 40, 43, 48 and the inside back cover; and Neville Stead for page 1 (photograph by V.E. Shelbourn) and pages 36 and 41 (photograph by N.W. Sprinks). The remaining photographs are from the author's and publisher's collections.

**The façade of the first Stevenage Station, 31 May 1973.
This closed in July the same year.**

INTRODUCTION

Hertfordshire during the Railway Age (which lasted roughly from 1850 to 1950) was not the faceless commuter suburb and new town sprawl of today's county. Until Victorian times the county was agricultural, the rolling countryside interspersed at regular intervals with small but historically interesting market towns. Except for the rapid development of Watford as an industrial suburb of London, the coming of the railways initially did little to change this. Essentially, the early main lines of the 1830s and '40s – the London & Birmingham, the Eastern Counties to Cambridge, and the Great Northern heading towards York – passed straight through. In the 1850s and '60s locally organised branch lines were spun off to the old market towns. Invariably these were worked from the outset by the main line companies which absorbed them inexpensively after a few years of unprofitable life. Latecomers – the Midland in the late 1860s, the Metropolitan twenty years later and the Great Northern's Hertford loop in the first quarter of the twentieth century – put most of these old towns on direct lines to London, while the branch lines continued in service for local traffic, especially from intermediate villages to the market towns. Perhaps the branch lines' prime importance was for goods, particularly deliveries to and from the light industrial sites which began to spring up on the edge of the towns from the turn of the twentieth century onwards.

By the time of the First World War the railway network in the county formed a tight grid. Running roughly north to south in a radial pattern out of London were the main lines and these were (clockwise): 1. Metropolitan & Great Central Joint (local services by the 'Met', Great Central to the Midlands); 2. London & North Western (successor to the London & Birmingham); 3. Midland Railway; 4. Great Northern main line; 5. Hertford loop (Great Northern alternative main line and a suburban 'might-have-been'*, completed 1924); 6. Great Eastern main line to Cambridge (formerly Eastern Counties). Between these were a series of mostly east–west oriented branch lines.

In 1923 the 200 or so old private railway companies in this country were reorganised into four new super companies. The London & North Western and Midland fell to the London, Midland and Scottish Railway (LMS) and the Great Central, Great Northern and Great Eastern to the London & North Eastern Railway (LNER). The Metropolitan survived as an independent company until 1933 when it became part of London Transport. These developments did not affect the services which continued very much as before until the whole rail network was nationalised as British Railways in 1948.

British Railways operated under severe financial restraints and within two decades the county's extensive network of branch lines had been severely pruned; only the Broxbourne–Hertford, Watford–St Albans and Moor Park–Watford branches survive. The closure of passenger services was obviously due to lack of use, but in the case of Hertfordshire the transfer of passengers was mostly to buses rather than cars as the branch lines were typically closed in the early '50s. In many ways the timing of closure was ironic as future suburban developments may have made many lines more viable. However the branch system could only have been rendered truly useful by a massive state-funded investment programme, something which, economically and politically, was simply not on the cards. Nevertheless it is pleasant to fantasise how agreeable it would be for modern Hertfordshire residents to be able to use a low-cost electric train on a cross-county ring railway, roughly following the route of the old south tier of branch lines, rather than the rowdy, death-dealing M25.

A train in open country near Hemel Hempstead. The photograph was taken from Adeyfield Road, now the site of a housing estate.

* It was intended that the Hertford loop would develop thriving commuter traffic, but this largely failed to materialise.

Aylesbury branch *

Passenger service withdrawn	2 February 1953	*Stations closed*	*Date*
Distance	6.9 miles	Marston Gate	2 February 1953
Company	London & North Western Railway		

Marston Gate Station, looking towards Aylesbury, 24 January 1953. The station buildings still exist, although they are much altered.

Only slightly more than two miles of this line lay in the tongue of Hertfordshire which protrudes up into Buckinghamshire. Promoted and built by the Aylesbury Railway – a company of local origin but firmly under the thumb of the London & Birmingham – the line was ceremonially opened on 10 June 1839. The Aylesbury Railway was built as the first section of a projected line to Oxford, but remained all its life a simple country branch line from the Euston–Birmingham main line at Cheddington to Aylesbury. The local company was absorbed into the London & North Western Railway, along with the London & Birmingham, in 1846.

* The closed station on this line that was in Buckinghamshire was Aylesbury High Street.

The rear of a push-pull train at Marston Gate Station, looking towards Cheddington on the same day as the previous photograph. These trains were used on several Hertfordshire branch lines.

The Aylesbury branch ran straight and level across the flat Vale of Aylesbury. It was primarily concerned with the transport of agricultural produce, especially milk from local dairy farms, but also supplied coal and other sundries to Aylesbury. The line was also used for transporting the products of Aylesbury's printing and brewing industries. Apart from the very earliest years the branch never saw intensive use and was an early victim of passenger closure. It remained open for goods until the end of 1963. Much of the route has been reabsorbed into the farmland on which it was built.

Braintree branch (Bishops Stortford to Braintree) *

Passenger service withdrawn	1 March 1952	* Closed stations on this line that were in Essex were Takeley, Easton
Distance	18 miles	Lodge, Dunmow, Felstead and Rayne.
Company	Great Eastern Railway	

About one mile of this straggling rural branch line was in Hertfordshire and there were no stations on that stretch of line. The line originated in a company called the Bishops Stortford, Dunmow & Braintree Railway. The branch opened on 22 February 1869, although by this time ownership had passed to the Great Eastern. Almost entirely dependent on agriculture, the only major centre of population served was the small town of Dunmow. The line was closed for goods in stages, the final movement being in 1972.

Buntingford branch

Passenger service withdrawn	16 November 1964	*Stations closed*	*Date*
Distance	13.8 miles	Hadham	16 November 1964
Company	Great Eastern Railway	Standon	16 November 1964
		Braughing	16 November 1964
Stations closed	*Date*	West Mill	16 November 1964
Mardock	16 November 1964	Buntingford	16 November 1964
Widford	16 November 1964		

Mardock Station, looking towards Buntingford, 2 June 1956.

Widford Station, looking towards Buntingford, 2 June 1956.

This line was different from the other Hertfordshire branches in several respects. Firstly, it was orientated along a north–south axis rather than east–west. Secondly, it was rather longer than the others. Thirdly, it served an area that industry failed to touch; in fact the line more resembles the straggling rural lines of East Anglia.

A former Great Eastern locomotive, No. 1154, at Hadham Station, May 1934.

One resemblance the line had with its counterparts, however, was in its origins. The good burghers of Buntingford desired a railway to connect their small town to the outside world and organising the Ware, Hadham & Buntingford Railway, they gained authorisation in 1858. Initially, as its title suggests, the junction was to have been at Ware, on what was to become the Great Eastern's Hertford branch, but this was soon changed to St Margaret's, one stop closer to London.

Locomotive No. 69685 at Hadham with the 2.28 p.m. from St Margaret's.

Capital was difficult to raise and the Eastern Counties Railway (which became part of the Great Eastern in 1862) stepped in. The line was opened on 3 July 1863. It went through rolling country of woods, meadows and fields and was noted for numerous bridges and steep grades. Its life as a nominally independent company was short and in 1868 it was merged into the Great Eastern, which had worked the line from the start.

Standon Station. The grounded coach was used for goods purposes.

Although the only major population centre served was the small market town of Buntingford, the branch seems to have been relatively well patronised. Through trains were operated to London and a substantial commuter traffic was established.

**Locomotive No. 69682 at Standon with the 2.26 p.m.
service from Buntingford, 2 June 1956.**

The line survived to be dieselised in 1959. However, through trains were discontinued at this time and this most probably led to decreased usage of the branch and subsequently to its closure five years later. Agricultural produce was the main source of goods traffic on the branch, although there was also a flour mill at Standon. The line was closed to freight in 1965.

Braughing Station.

Looking toward Buntingford at Braughing Station, 2 June 1956.

Buntingford Station, 16 April 1957. The building was the combined station house and booking office.

An early view of Buntingford Station.

Locomotive No. 69682 at Buntingford with the 2.26 p.m.
to St Margaret's. The photograph was not dated.

Croxley Green branch (Watford High Street Junction to Croxley Green)

Passenger service withdrawn	22 March 1996	*Stations closed*	*Date*
Distance	1.8 miles	Watford Stadium	22 March 1996
Company	London & North Western Railway	Watford West	22 March 1996
		Croxley Green	22 March 1996

Watford West Station, 31 May 1966. This station served the outskirts of the town.

This short branch was built by the London & North Western as part of its 'New Lines' scheme, a project aimed at providing a new double track line for suburban services. For good measure the company threw in a branch towards the village of Croxley Green, which split from the Rickmansworth branch at Croxley Green Junction and ran around the outskirts of Watford to its terminus on Rickmansworth Road.

Croxley Green Station, photographed not long after it opened.

The branch was essentially a speculative venture to cash in on what promised to be a major commuter area. The line was in cutting except for the terminal and its approaches, which included a substantial bridge over the Grand Union Canal. The branch was opened for passengers on 15 June 1912. Steam trains were used until electrification was completed on 30 October 1922. Passenger traffic was not as great as had been anticipated, but generous services were provided until the outbreak of war in 1939. The branch's slow decline was not reversed by the opening of a halt serving Watford football ground in 1982. It remained officially open for several years after the last train ran in 1996, the few passengers carried by a replacement bus service. The passenger withdrawal included a section of the Rickmansworth branch from High Street Junction to Croxley Green Junction. Goods traffic had played a very minor role and had been withdrawn by the end of 1966. Currently, there are plans to build a new line to connect the old Croxley branch to the Watford branch to enable Metropolitan trains to run through to Watford Junction Station.

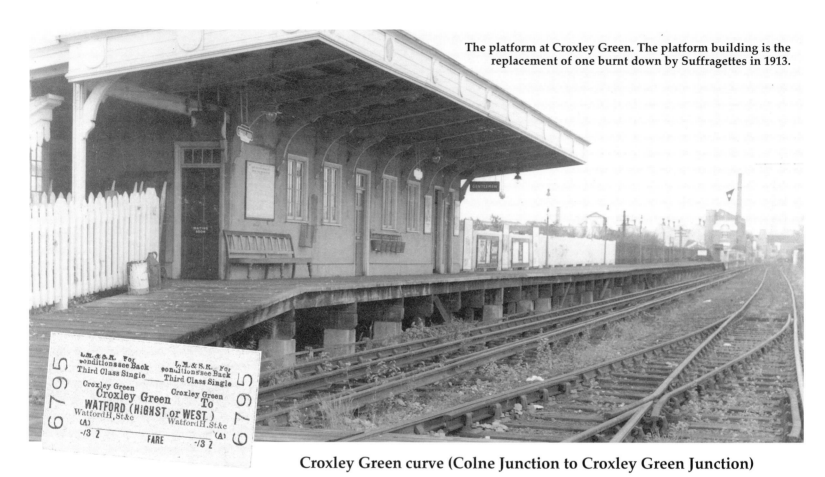

The platform at Croxley Green. The platform building is the replacement of one burnt down by Suffragettes in 1913.

Croxley Green curve (Colne Junction to Croxley Green Junction)

Passenger service withdrawn	6 June 1966
Distance	0.4 miles
Company	London & North Western Railway

This spur, originally and more picturesquely referred to as the Tumbling Bay loop, was built to allow Croxley Green commuters to travel directly to London via Bushey without changing at Watford. Such services began on 30 October 1922, when the Croxley Green branch was electrified, but the curve may well have been in occasional use before that time. The line was entirely embankment except for the bridge across Wiggenhall Road. The Croxley Green branch was never particularly well patronised and it is surprising that the direct service continued as long as it did. The last train was on 6 June 1966, but the official date of closure was on 19 September of that year. The curve was seldom if ever used for goods purposes. The old embankment remains in place and can be seen from the windows of trains running between Bushey and Watford High Street.

Dunstable branch *

Passenger service withdrawn	24 April 1965	*Stations closed*	*Date*
Distance	19.3 miles	Welwyn Junction	1 September 1860
Company	Great Northern Railway	Welwyn Garden City	20 September 1926
		Ayot	29 September 1949
* Closed stations on this line that were in Bedfordshire were Luton		Wheathampstead	24 April 1965
Hoo, Luton Bute Street, Dunstable Town and Dunstable North.		Harpenden (East)	24 April 1965

**The second Welwyn Garden City Station opened in 1926 and is still in use.
The nearest platform was used by Dunstable branch trains.**

A Stephenson Locomotive Society rail tour from Hatfield to Dunstable, passing Ayot Station signal box, 14 April 1962.

The Great Northern's Dunstable branch, about eleven miles of which was in Hertfordshire, originated in the desire of Luton's business elite to connect the town to the country's railway network. The Luton, Dunstable & Welwyn Junction Railway projected two routes: one north to the railhead of the London & North Western's Dunstable branch; the other, which concerns us here, south to join the Great Northern near Welwyn.

Wheathampstead Station.

The northern line went rapidly ahead and was completed in 1858. The southern one opened on 1 September 1860. By this time the LD&WJ had merged with the company responsible for building the Great Northern's Hertford branch, forming the Hertford, Luton & Dunstable Railway. This company seems to have wanted to keep its lines from the clutches of the Great Northern and constructed the approaches to what would have been a bridge over the Great Northern main line north of the future Welwyn Garden City Station. The main line corporation appears to have balked at this and absorbed the impecunious HL&DR in 1861. The route was built cheaply due to lack of need for extensive earthworks. Before 1868 Luton trains used the main line tracks to the junction station at Hatfield.

Wheathampstead Station around 1905.

When the Midland opened its line to London in 1868 the branch lost its essential raison d'étre. Although times to London from Luton remained competitive well into the twentieth century, the line became much like any other rural branch line. Passenger numbers, mostly comprised of commuters from the small towns of Wheathampstead and Harpenden, remained relatively large into the 1950s. However, car usage took its toll and despite the introduction of diesel haulage the branch was closed for passengers. The most famous user of the line was George Bernard Shaw who was a regular at Wheathampstead.

Harpenden Station, *c.*1930.

Goods traffic was mainly to and from Luton and Dunstable, although the Hertfordshire stretch did contribute as agricultural produce, especially salad vegetables, was carried from market gardening areas around Harpenden and Wheathampstead. The latter also had a chemical factory. The building of the garden city at Welwyn also created a certain amount of trade. However, it was Blackbridge siding (near Ayot), first serving gravel pits and later a rubbish dump, that was most important. After the line's closure to general goods in 1966, traffic continued to the dump until 1971. Part of the old route is now a country walk and substantial sections have been used for road improvements or reclaimed for agriculture.

A double-headed goods train passing Harpenden, 5 September 1959.

Hemel Hempstead branch

			Stations closed	Date
Passenger service withdrawn		16 June 1947	Redbourn	16 June 1947
Distance		8.1 miles	Beaumonts Halt	16 June 1947
Company		Midland Railway	Godwin's Halt	16 June 1947
			Hemel Hempstead	16 June 1947
Stations closed		*Date*	Heath Park Halt	16 June 1947
Roundwood Halt		16 June 1947		

A Midland & Great Northern 4-4-0T, with a Pullman coach, at the Midland Railway's station at Harpenden. This locomotive was temporarily on loan to the Midland and is at the bay platform used by branch trains. This station opened on 13 July 1868 and is still in use.

Roundwood Halt, with an LMS 'Hawkseye' sign.

The Midland's Hemel Hempstead branch had its origins in a locally organised company. The title of the Hemel Hempsted (*sic*) & London & North Western Railway sums up its aim – to connect the little market town to the Euston main line near Boxmoor (now Hemel Hempstead) Station. The Parliamentary act was passed in 1863 but the London & North Western showed no enthusiasm. They already had a station serving the area and felt that a short branch line to what was hardly more than a large village, whose main 'industry' was straw plaiting, was not worth the bother. However, the HH&LNW started work anyway.

Redbourn Station, 1938. The wooden station building was identical to the one at Hemel Hempstead.

In 1866 the HH&LNW gained authorisation to join the Great Northern's Dunstable branch at Harpenden, but the Great Northern also had second thoughts and the Midland stepped in. After considerable delay the line was ceremonially opened on 16 July 1877. The local company was absorbed by the Midland in 1886.

Beaumont's Halt, looking towards Harpenden, 5 September 1959.

Known locally as 'the Nickey line' (although nobody can be exactly sure what this name refers to), the branch had severe gradients and numerous bridges. The branch was never very well used by passengers. Choosing the Midland to go to London from Hemel was a roundabout route (particularly before 1888 when Luton rather than Harpenden was the junction for the branch). Intermediate traffic too was scarce – the small village of Redbourn was originally the only other stop.

Godwin's Halt, looking east around 1950.

In 1905 the Midland turned to operation by steam railmotor (a peculiar contraption – essentially a light locomotive embedded in the front part of a carriage), hoping a tram-like service would boost usage. Three unstaffed halts with short wooden platforms were opened (a fourth was added later). Another oddity, the Ro-Railer, an experimental bus-train hybrid, operated on the branch briefly in the early 1930s. In the event nothing could save the line, particularly after a parallel bus service was introduced.

Hemel Hempstead Station, *c.*1914. The Midland Hotel (not railway owned) in the background still stands.

Goods traffic was dominated by coal for domestic use as well as supplies to the gas works at Boxmoor. Early on most outward trade was agricultural. Later, gravel extraction and brick-making became the mainstays. After closure for general goods in the mid 1960s, Hemelite, a breeze block manufacturer, continued to use part of the line until the junction was clipped out in 1979 for operational reasons connected with the electrification of the Midland main line.

Locomotive No. 1669 at Hemel Hempstead with the 2.37 p.m. service for Harpenden, 19 October 1929. Note the antique spelling of the town.

The line was removed in stages, the southern part being redeveloped from 1960 whereas track was not removed from the last section until 1982. Although large sections of the alignment have been built over, the remainder is in use as a footpath.

The Ro-Railer at Hemel Hempstead, 1931.

A steam railmotor at Heath Park Halt. The location is now the site of Hemel's famous 'Magic Roundabout'.

Hertford branch

		Stations closed	Date
Passenger service withdrawn	Hertford North – Cowbridge: 1 June 1924; Hatfield – Hertford North: 18 June 1951	Welwyn Garden City	20 September 1926
		Hatfield Hyde	1 July 1905
Distance	10 miles	Attimore Halt	1 July 1905
Company	Great Northern Railway	Cole Green	18 June 1951
		Hertingfordbury	18 June 1951
		Hertford Cowbridge	1 June 1924

Welwyn Garden City Station.

This branch had origins that will already be familiar: the elite of a small town organised a company to build a branch which they hoped would reinvigorate their slightly mouldy market town. In this case the Hertford & Welwyn Junction Railway was to connect the county town with the Great Northern main line. The line opened on 1 March 1858 and ran through pretty, if undistinguished, countryside to terminate alongside the River Lea. Through running with the Great Eastern was contemplated and there was a link beyond Cowbridge Station, but this appears never to have been used for passenger services.

Attimore Halt was open for only six months between January 1905 and 1 July the same year.

Initially, the junction station was at Welwyn, but from 1860 trains ran through to Hatfield over the main line (a single track line for branch use parallel to the main line along this section was in use from 1876). The Hertford company amalgamated with the concern which had built what became the Great Northern's Dunstable branch shortly after opening. This new company, the Hertford, Luton & Dunstable, had a short life as it merged with the Great Northern in 1861. The line originally had some local traffic from the villages of Cole Green and Hertingfordbury to the market towns of Hatfield and Hertford, but such trade was largely stolen by parallel bus services from 1921 onwards. During the nineteenth and early twentieth centuries the branch was fairly well used for passengers to London, although a change was usually necessary. However, completion of the Hertford loop line in 1924, offering direct services to London, robbed the branch of any commuter potential.

Class G2 0-4-4WT, No. 531, at Cole Green Station. The locomotive was built in 1875 and was fairly typical of the type used on the GNR branch lines before grouping.

Upon the opening of the loop Hertford branch trains terminated at the new Hertford North Station, Cowbridge being closed except for goods. This development lowered the passenger potential of the branch further as the new station was even further away from the town centre than the old one, so it is not surprising that the branch was an early victim of passenger closure. Goods traffic was of the usual general nature, including domestic coal. In later years considerable trips were made to a dump at Cole Green. The line was closed for general goods traffic in 1966, but a short section at the western end remained in use until 1982 serving factories on the outskirts of Welwyn Garden City. Some sections of the old branch have been built on, but the bulk remains as a public footpath.

Hertingfordbury Station, 9 September 1962.

Hitchin branch (Bedford to Hitchin) *

Passenger service withdrawn	1 January 1962	
Distance	16 miles	
Company	Midland Railway	

* Closed stations on this line that were in Bedfordshire were Henlow, Shefford, Southill and Cardington.

Before it built its own line into London, the Midland ran via the Great Northern into Kings Cross. The line from Leicestershire to Hitchin, which allowed the Midland access to London, opened on 8 May 1857, although through running into Kings Cross did not start until the following year. After the opening of St Pancras in 1868, the main line to which branched off at Bedford, this section became the Midland's Hitchin branch. The line was singled in 1912 and although relatively well used, closed for passengers in 1962. About three miles of the branch was in Hertfordshire and there were no stations on that stretch.

Rickmansworth branch

Passenger service withdrawn	3 March 1952	*Stations closed*	*Date*
Distance	3 miles	Rickmansworth	3 March 1952
Company	London & North Western Railway		

Seen here on 25 August 1951, Rickmansworth Station had been renamed Rickmansworth Church Street the previous year. The station building had been rebuilt in the 1920s.

The Watford & Rickmansworth Railway was promoted by a consortium of local landowners headed by Lord Ebury of Moor Park. The intention was to further local development by creating a link between the London & North Western at Watford and the Great Western at Uxbridge, but extension beyond Rickmansworth never materialised. Construction was costly – the rivers Colne, Chess and Gade and the Grand Union Canal had to be bridged – but not lengthy and the line opened on 1 October 1862, less than two years after authorisation. It was worked from the start by the London & North Western which took over the local company in 1881. The line was electrified as part of the London & North Western's suburban development programme in 1927.

Rickmansworth Church Street, 28 June 1951.

Passenger traffic was gradually eaten away – the coming of the Metropolitan to Rickmansworth in 1887 robbed the line of its London trade and buses from the 1920s onwards took most of the rest. As a result the line was an early victim of passenger closure, although goods traffic remained considerable. Watercress was carried from Rickmansworth from early on, but industrial sidings to the west of Watford were more important. Coal went to Watford's municipally-run power station, and coal and salt to Eastbury pumping station via a privately-owned two foot gauge light railway. A long siding was laid to Croxley Mill (a paper works) for deliveries of coal and other supplies. This last remained in use until 1983, although general goods services to Rickmansworth had ceased on 2 January 1967. Most of the old line can be walked and many bridges are still in place. Part of the Watford & Rickmansworth Railway was double-tracked in 1912 and remains in use for the Euston–Watford d.c. electric trains. This includes Watford High Street Station, originally the intermediate station on the line.

St Albans branch

Passenger service withdrawn	1 October 1951	*Stations closed*	*Date*
Distance	6.5 miles	Lemsford Road Halt	1 October 1951
Company	Great Northern Railway	Nast Hyde Halt	1 October 1951
		Smallford	1 October 1951
		Hill End	1 October 1951
		St Albans (London Road)	1 October 1951

Smallford Station, *c.*1904. All the buildings seen here are still in use.

Like the Watford & Rickmansworth Railway this line had its origins as a local company, the Hatfield & St Albans Railway, which was organised by a group of landowners headed by Lord Ebury. In this case the strategic interests of the parent organisation – the Great Northern – were of paramount importance. In 1858 the London & North Western had opened a branch from Watford Junction to St Albans via Bricket Wood. This had robbed the Great Northern of the trade from the old cathedral town – Hatfield being formerly the railhead for St Albans. Oddly enough given the line's origins, trains were to terminate at the London & North Western's station, now St Albans Abbey. The line ran through easy countryside and so required little heavy construction. The line was opened on 16 October 1865, without great ceremonies which were rather passé by this time. As a ploy to win back custom the line was a great failure, for the Midland Railway's direct line to London was opened less than three years later. The local company was heavily financed by the main line corporation, the line was always worked by it and was absorbed by it in 1883.

Passenger usage was always fairly light. There was a certain amount of end-to-end traffic – shoppers, workers and schoolchildren – however, the countryside between the two towns was lightly populated and despite attempts to boost commuter traffic London-bound traffic from St Albans mostly went to St Pancras. Bus competition began to bite in the thirties and despite a temporary revival during the Second World War, caused especially by workers travelling to the De Havilland works in Hatfield, by the end of the 1940s trains were mostly running empty. The last passenger train ran on 28 September 1951. Goods traffic was particularly varied on this line. Agricultural produce, especially potatoes, was carried, as was that other standard, domestic coal. At Butterwick (between Smallford and Hill End) a siding served a meat store and banana warehouse built during the Second World War. This was a good source of traffic in later years. At Hill End a spur led into the Herts. County Mental Hospital for deliveries of coal and general supplies. Nearby was a railway-connected brick works, closed around 1940. The Salvation Army's printing works near St Albans was particularly important: *War Cry* was produced here and sent over the line for distribution. An unusual traffic was in orchids grown at Sanders' Nurseries on the outskirts of St Albans. These flowers, the vital addition to the Edwardian gentleman's buttonhole, were transported in specially designed vans. General goods traffic ceased on 5 October 1964, although workings continued to various sidings along the line until 1968. This is one of the best preserved of the old branch lines. The trackbed has been converted into a footpath and cycle-track which, apart from a few breaks at either end, can be walked from St Albans to Hatfield.

Watford North curve (Watford North to Watford East Junction)

Passenger service withdrawn   4 January 1960   *Company*   Metropolitan & London &
Distance   0.8 miles   North Eastern Joint Committee

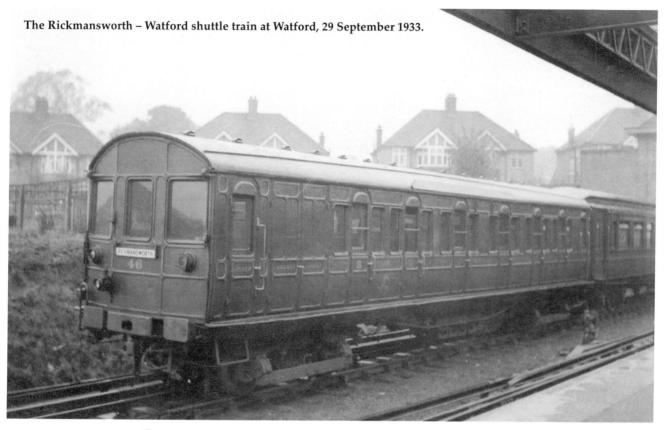

The Rickmansworth – Watford shuttle train at Watford, 29 September 1933.

This short connecting line opened on 2 November 1925, at the same time as the Watford branch of what is now the Metropolitan Line, and was constructed to allow a direct Rickmansworth to Watford service. This was provided by Metropolitan Railway electric trains on a shuttle basis. The regular service was withdrawn on 1 January 1934 in the face of fierce bus competition but was reinstated on a limited basis in 1941. The line was in use for goods purposes until 1966 and continues in use for empty stock transfers only.

Closed passenger stations on lines still open to passengers

Cambridge main line (Great Eastern Railway)

Stations closed   *Date*

* Station resited: replacement currently open.

Stations closed	Date
Waltham Cross *	1 January 1885
Cheshunt *	1 October 1891

Great Northern Railway main line

* Station resited: replacement currently open.

Stations closed
Welwyn Junction
Stevenage *

Date
1 September 1860
23 July 1973

Class E2 208 series No. 711 arriving at Stevenage Station. The building seen here is the original of 1850 and was replaced around 1895.

Stevenage Station.

Stapleford Station, 9 June 1932.

London & North Western Railway main line
* Station resited: replacement currently open.

London & North Western local line
* Station resited: replacement currently open.

Stations closed	*Date*
Watford *	4 May 1858
Berkhampstead *	1875

Stations closed	*Date*
Carpenters Park *	17 November 1952

Carpenter's Park Station, 25 August 1951. The old station was just to the north of the present one.